STOP THE MUSICAL RIDE, I WANT OFF!

1972
GRAY'S PUBLISHING LTD.
SIDNEY, B.C.

100 YEARS IN THE R.C.M.P. SADDLE! OR, STOP THE MUSICAL RIDE, I WANT OFF!

CARTOONS BY FRANK SPALDING

Copyright © 1972 by Frank S. Spalding

Designed and printed by the
MORRISS PRINTING COMPANY LTD.
Victoria, British Columbia

FOREWORD

IF ANYONE TRIES TO POSE AS a member of the Force and *cannot* give his Regimental Number, he *must* be an imposter. So let us set *this* record straight!

Regimental Number 11764 decided to publish Regimental Number 11745's cartoons, notes and anecdotes to celebrate the one hundredth anniversary of the finest body of men in the world. Regimental Number 11745 was born into the Force, his father having helped make much of the early history before retiring as Deputy Commissioner J. W. Spalding.

Regimental Number 11745 recently retired as Assistant Commissioner Frank S. Spalding and those of us who served in the early thirties remember him as a fellow constable. And one of Frank's sons continued the tradition into the third generation.

With recent criticism and an apparently organized attack on one of our *last* Canadian traditions, it seems fitting to show the Service, the last one remaining, as it sees itself — its humour, inside jokes and the building of a tradition most Canadians would *like* to cherish.

Many ex-members will identify with or recall actual events during the golden years of their youth. So here it is, warts and all, presented with affection.

Stop The Musical Ride, I Want Off!

INTRODUCTION

COMRADES IN THE FORCE, and civilian friends, produced some very attractive titles for this little book during the past two years of its evolution. Such captions as *Funny Men in Red*, *Sex in the Saddle* and *Sex and the Single Mountie* really intrigued me for, apart from their suggestive quality, they may have had great sales appeal. However, long formative years in the disciplined embrace of the Royal Canadian Mounted, before and after enlistment, proved *too* inhibiting. I say *before* because I was born into the Force in the old Royal North-West Mounted Police barracks at Calgary, Alberta, in 1910, where my father was the Post Sergeant-Major.

The acquisition of a sense of humour must have come from some of my Irish forbears on mother's side, I don't really know, but it was disturbing to some that the occasional scenes of pomp and ceremony, parades, etc., used to strike me as funny. You will see what I mean further on in these pages.

After running off dozens of thoughts and suggestions, an eye-catching title still eluded me for months. This prompted a reporter acquaintance of mine to comment that he firmly believed *all* policemen lacked a sense of humour. Suppressing an urge to react violently, I glibly suggested that he ask for a sabbatical year, then go and *serve* on police beat in Montreal or Vancouver, or an R.C.M.P. detachment. "There," he cried, "you *just* proved my point."

However, a young man who is a book designer, Bev Leech by name, after looking at the cartoons, suggested: *Stop The Musical Ride, I Want Off!* ... *Bingo*, that was it!

Policemen the world over are *people*, a fact which seems to have been overlooked by many today, and people *can* be funny!

In any military or paramilitary environment, the provocation for mirth is frequently induced by peculiarities relating to form and tradition. Happenings which might be hilarious to a soldier may look or sound absolutely incongruous to the outsider. Of course such idiosyncrasies apply to other walks of life, but the "Achilles Heel" of pomp, discipline and rigidity renders the services more vulnerable in the breach and can evoke laughter often far beyond the quality of the incident. In this light I considered it essential to write short narratives to explain *some* of the illustrations.

During thirty-six years of service in the Royal Canadian Mounted Police, when there was time, I played a little tennis, became fairly proficient on the horizontal bar, did a little boxing before and after enlistment and played football and rugger. But I do not regard such activities as "hobbies." My only one, in truth, was sketching and cartooning.

Throughout these years I cartooned perhaps thousands of happenings and incidents, with not a few caricatures of some personalities, such as policemen, judges, lawyers and politicians. The vast majority of these were given away upon request. Some got me into trouble, but most were cheerfully accepted. A few of the originals were retained, others found their way into the *Royal Canadian Mounted Police Quarterly*, the regimental voice of the Force and one of the best publications in Canada. Some of the *original* cartoons appear in this book and are so delineated.

Of these years in the police environment, I served nearly sixteen in what is known as "other ranks," that is from constable to senior non-commissioned officer. This involved "General Duty," a Mounted Police terminology which in essence is active service. However, it formerly covered a *multitude* of assignments. Anything from being nursemaid to a horse, mucking out stables, polishing brass, escorting prisoners, handling dogs, counting migratory birds and animals, guarding V.I.P.'s to investigating all types of crime from chicken stealing to murder.

These were truly the formative years, for, while still a bachelor they took me to northern Saskatchewan, the Arctic and the provinces of Ontario and Quebec. I rapidly learned many things: how *not* to paddle a canoe; how *not* to ride a cowpony with an R.C.M.P. bridle and bit; how to drive a car on a "gumbo" road; how to make a high speed about face on dry pavement without upsetting the police car; how to chase a get-away car on a dry gravel road and not be blinded by dust or have your windshield smashed by stones. And about people: Never judge a man by his appearance. Brains, intelligence and social position are little protection against the wiles of a really good con man. That some people can be unbelievably cruel and vicious, even the press will not publish the anatomies of some murders. That some criminals are not all bad; even under stress of apprehension they have a wry sense of humour. Lastly, that a life of celibacy is not all it is cracked up to be; either in the Mounted Police or the priesthood, so . . .

I met a dear little blond girl in Ottawa while on temporary duty there and five years later married her when I was a Lance Corporal. Our first son, Jim, was born in Quebec. A second son, Frank, was born in Saskatchewan when I was a full Corporal (confirmed sounds better), and lastly, a beautiful little girl, Sandra, was born to us in Manitoba. The advent of a second woman in my life must have been a good omen, for I was promoted to Sergeant not too long afterwards.

Fortune seemed to rear its beautiful head again, for a couple of years later I was promoted to commissioned rank (Sub-Inspector). The then Governor-General of Canada, Viscount Alexander of Tunis, signed my commission under the Great Seal of Canada. Few if any other police forces in the Commonwealth see their personnel commissioned from the ranks as is the case in the R.C.M.P.

As the years progressed I eventually saw service in almost all the provinces of Canada, from tiny hamlets on the prairies and the Maritimes to cities such as Halifax, Montreal, Quebec, Winnipeg, Regina and Victoria.

In spite of increased responsibilities as an officer, a few cartoons still appeared from my pen, albeit not so prolifically as in the past, due in part to mounds of paperwork and the rather austere environment of the officer hierarchy.

The illustrations and narratives which follow portray situations and predicaments in a serio-comic vein and, except for the historic pieces, I was and am familiar with through personal involvement.

For the 100th birthday of the Force I want to share with comrades, veterans and all good Canadians amusing or interesting incidents over the century.

A BIT OF HISTORY

In MAY OF 1973, officers and men of the Royal Canadian Mounted Police, veterans and former members, will pause to look back over the long patrol of one hundred years marking the Force's history. They can do so with tremendous pride and no little affection in its achievement and the part, large or small, which each man played in the building and furtherance of the reputation and tradition.

It was in the year 1873 that the young government of Canada, after a somewhat lengthy conception, gave birth to the North-West Mounted Police. This offspring of law and justice proved both in infancy and adolescence, to be a child of reckless courage and naivete. Naive in the ways of war "Indian style," but *incredibly* lucky; ultimate maturity was accelerated dangerously by the confrontation in 1876 with the great Sitting Bull, mighty "medicine man" of the Sioux and nemesis of Custer and his 7th United States Cavalry. It was at this point in time, however, that the Force demonstrated to the world that courage and fortitude tempered with human understanding, tact and diplomacy, neutralized the gun and the lance.

Although the North-West Mounted of that day was a paramilitary body in structure and accoutrement, apart from a few of their leaders only nine were former soldiers out of an initial strength of approximately two hundred and forty-five. The majority, too, were Canadians from Ontario and Quebec with such former occupations as clerks, tradesmen, farmers, students and lumbermen.

These were ordinary men seeking at the outset adventure and change in the challenge of, even then, a rapidly shrinking frontier. But they became extraordinary men with amazing rapidity, in spite of a few desertions, extremely primitive living conditions and poor equipment. This conglomerate, nevertheless, made their presence felt on the western plains for peace, not war.

The Canadian and American Indians were quick to show their respect for courage, especially the variety which this small band of white men displayed on many a tension filled confrontation with the painted warriors of the plains. But what won the Indian almost completely was the restraint, tact and absolute impartiality shown by the Police, especially in the persons of leaders like Walsh and MacLeod.

Many contemporary historians, writers and newsmen in dealing with western Canadian history, do so out of context. They seem to ignore the fact that inter-tribal warfare was a way of life with the plains Indians and had been long before the "white eyes" marched in. Also, that on the Canadian scene in the early days they outnumbered the whites more than ten to one.

South of the border, however, the white man had continually demonstrated his own greed and perfidy by cheating and hounding the tribes, killing their old men, women and children, regardless of solemn treaties.

Canada was on the verge of this type of scurrilous development by the illegal immigration of whisky traders and outlaws who were in the process of despoiling the Canadian Indians, until the advent of the North-West Mounted.

The Mounted Police dealt with the lawless white element with alacrity and a forcefulness that would make some contemporary civil liberty advocates howl. But notwithstanding the impact of this gloved fist, justice was not only done, but seen to be done, especially by the Indian.

There was little if any resort to gunplay; indeed, the use of firearms was regarded with displeasure by the Force then, as it is now. No gunfighter made the scene on the Canadian plains; no vigilante riders nor lynch mobs rode at will. There were no sheriffs, marshals or deputies. There were *no* Earps, Dillons, Doc Hollidays, Billy the Kids or Bat Mastersons in western Canada! Such lawmen were neither needed nor would their presence have been tolerated by the North-West Mounted Police. I appreciate that this fact must irk television script writers and authors no end, but they can thank the Force for the dearth of such material.

They and the politicians should also be grateful to the Force that Canada was spared the terrible cost in blood and money of the grim Indian warfare that plagued the United States for many years.

Of course, the cynic will point to the Riel episode of 1885. Well it is not my desire, in a little publication of this type, to go into detailed history, but the record and the evidence of the day will clearly reveal that the Mounted Police had, long before 1885, reported to the government some of the dire problems and injustices which were weighing upon the Indians and Metis, but without result. When the fighting did begin the N.W.M.P. suffered almost as many casualties as the army, indeed on a percentage basis, they were greater; they did *far* more gruelling work.

Finally on this point, the blood-letting in the so-called Northwest Rebellion, and the financial cost, in terms of time and numbers involved, was a mere drop compared to the long and sanguinary Indian wars in the western states.

In conclusion then, why was the North-West Mounted Police Force able to accomplish such a feat as the peace-keeping in the Canadian west both before and after this rebellion? To view the whole panorama one must read history, in particular; *History of the North-West Mounted Police* by J. P. Turner; *Policing* the *Plains* by R. G. MacBeth and the *Royal Canadian Mounted Police* by R. C. Fetherstonaugh. But the most exciting and interesting, in my opinion, is T. M. Longstreth's, *The Silent Force*. These are but a few of the more than *thirty* books written about the Force.

Briefly then, the success of the early Force was based in the main upon a high standard of leadership and strict discipline, plus a display of excellent personal initiative by all ranks. But also in terms of growth and development of the country, the men of the Mounted Police, by their detached patrolling and the manning of remote posts, became part and parcel of the frontier community, working *with* people of all stations.

They distributed food to starving Indian bands, or guided them to new hunting grounds. They aided struggling settlers, performed rescue missions, fought prairie fires and often tended the sick and injured, both white and Indian. They carried the mail, acted as coroners and buried the dead. In essence the daily lives of the majority of the men of the Force were bound up with the people they served.

This relationship, this communication if you will, constituted the policy of the North-West, Royal North-West and Royal Canadian Mounted Police.

The Force initially paved the way for full settlement and made the path safe for ranchers, farmers, doctors and lawyers, not to mention the building of the Canadian Pacific Railway.

The contemporary scene has changed to this extent — the modern "Mounted Policeman" functions under conditions totally unknown to his predecessor. His role is infinitely more complex and sophisticated in many ways; surprisingly to some, even more dangerous! Rapid transportation and communication, plus the glare of the public spotlight through the mass medias, illuminates his slightest error in judgment, frequently enlarging it out of all proportion to that error.

Politicians are more interested now, not necessarily in his welfare, but in his operations. But the worst feature of all in today's climate finds the Royal Canadian Mounted Policeman along with *all* policemen, being subjected to the continuous outpouring of criticism mixed with vilification and abuse. To paraphrase, never have so few (in the public service) been *criticized* by so many!

Nevertheless the officers and men of the present day Royal Canadian Mounted Police, standing as they do on the threshold of one hundred years of service, have proven conclusively, even to the most caustic and petulant critic, that this unique Force is the honour guard of peace and a recognized symbol of Canada. Also they are synonymous with their predecessors of 1873, in terms of courage, discipline and integrity.

SOME CONTEMPORARY WRITERS and commentators seem inclined to confine the salient points of Mounted Police history to the long march west in 1874; the occupation of the notorious but undefended Fort Whoop-Up in the same year, and the Battle of Duck Lake in 1885.

Without minimizing the significance of these occurrences, the actual "moment of truth" in terms of potential disaster, prolonged peril and tension, began at a point in time three years after the official establishment of the North-West Mounted Police in 1873.

The crucial year was 1876, and the principals involved were Superintendent James Morrow Walsh of the North-West Mounted, and *Ta-tan-ka Yo tan-ki*, or Sitting Bull, the intelligent and politically powerful Medicine Man of the fighting Sioux. He was not only a diplomat, but a strategist who achieved the unprecedented unity of the Cheyennes and the Ogalalla Sioux. And then master-minded the total defeat of Lieutenant-Colonel George A. Custer and the U.S. 7th Cavalry at the Little Big Horn, June 25th, 1876. Bull then carried out an amazing withdrawal of not only his warriors, but also the old men, women and children, successfully evading fresh and numerically superior U.S. forces hard on his trail. The Sioux travelled north into Canadian territory, eventually camping in the vicinity of Fort Walsh, the North-West Mounted Police headquarters at that time.

Soon after this Sitting Bull, the proud victor, and James Morrow Walsh, the tough, courageous and straight-talking Mounted Police officer, met. He was one of the originals of the Force; a strict disciplinarian but scrupulously fair and just. These outstanding traits impressed not only his *own* men, but more importantly, the Sioux.

Sitting Bull, at this moment in history, held all the cards in terms of numbers, experience and firepower. There were over two thousand men, women and children in the tribes; more than eight hundred of whom were seasoned scalp-carrying warriors.

This capability was augmented by battlefield plunder, which included quantities of ammunition, hundreds of horses and mules, and general supplies taken from Custer's command.

Superintendent Walsh, on the other hand, was backed by less than a hundred lightly armed members of the North-West Mounted Police, housed in a not too substantial fort.

The police officer and the Indian leader, Sitting Bull, in their initial confrontation, exchanged harsh words and voiced threats; but both knew that the Sioux warriors were fully capable of responding instantly to the war cry of their chief, and attacking Fort Walsh. Regardless of desperate and courageous resistance, the Mounted Police would have been exterminated.

Fortunately, Superintendent Walsh so impressed Sitting Bull with his courage and impartiality, that in the tension filled months that followed, the Sioux leader found a grudging admiration for the white police officer. This, in turn, developed into respect and mutual friendship which lasted throughout their lives.

I commend to the media seekers after "Canadian content" in the realm of adventure, that they examine some of the books about the Mounted Police including one written by the Canadian authoress, Iris Allan, entitled *White Sioux*; also John Peter Turner's *History of the North-West Mounted Police*.

The pen and wash drawing opposite, shows Superintendent James M. Walsh and Sitting Bull, with Fort Walsh in the background.

THERE HAVE ALWAYS BEEN *many* outstanding men in the Royal Canadian Mounted Police in terms of gallantry, or distinguished service to the Force and country.

It is therefore difficult in a limited production such as this, to portray any *one* individual. However, I'm sure that my comrades in the Force past and present, will agree with the inclusion of my friend, the late Superintendent Henry Asbjorn Larsen, F.R.G.S., who enlisted in the R.C.M.P. in 1928 and retired in 1961. In addition to his Second World War medals, Larsen held the Massey Medal of the Royal Canadian Geographical Society, the Polar Medal and Bar. He was also a Fellow of the Arctic Institute of North America, and an honourary member of the Royal Geographical Society, holding the Patron's Gold Medal of this Society.

These honours were given for Henry's work in Canada's Arctic regions and for his navigational and exploratory efforts while in command of the R.C.M.P. motor schooner, *St. Roch*. Larsen, his crew and vessel were the *first* to sail the Northwest Passage, *west to east*, from Vancouver to Halifax in the hazardous Arctic Ocean. This voyage took from June 1940 to October 1942 and was one of great hardship and danger due to extremely adverse weather and ice conditions.

Later, in July of 1944, to October the same year, the little police schooner made the return voyage from Halifax, N.S., to Vancouver, B.C. The *first* ship in history to make the journey *both* ways!

These voyages were all the more remarkable when one considers the size of the *St. Roch*, the small complement of her crew, and the *particular* years involved. The vessel was built in Burrard shipyard, North Vancouver, 1928. She is 104 feet long with a 25-foot beam; made of Douglas Fir and Australian iron-bark. She was powered by diesel engines.

No man succeeds in such a monumental undertaking alone, and Henry Larsen always acknowledged and paid tribute to his gallant crew, all of whom were members, non-commissioned officers and constables of the R.C.M. P.

A native of Norway, Larsen was a rugged and determined man but possessed of a most infectious good humoured grin. He loved the Eskimo people, and they, him. He lived in their camps on his many arctic patrols and shared their food. He spoke on their behalf in government circles, long before it became the "in thing".

Superintendent Larsen died in 1964, shortly after his 65th birthday.

North-West Mounted Constable: "But Chief, I want to marry your daughter."

Blackfoot Chief: "Red Coat know Great White Mother's Law say him *no* take squaw for *seven years.* You join Blackfoot *now*, or come back in seven years."

WHEN THEY WERE HARD PRESSED FOR FOOD, particularly fresh meat, some of the Plains Indian tribes indulged in dog meat. This development occurred when the vast herds of buffalo were being rapidly depleted.

Here we see a lone North-West Mounted constable having a rest in an Indian encampment after having partaken of a meal at the invitation of the Chief.

Constable: "That was heap good Chief, what was it?"

Chief: "Red Coat please excuse pun, but I heard it from a white eye who used to bring firewater into camp — you just had a little bit of the hair of that dog that — Ho ho ho! Ugh, you get *rest* of it?"

Constable: "*Ho ho,* I get it Chief — excuse me *too*, while I go behind teepee."

THE SHOW OFF?

THE FOLLOWING IS AN EXTRACT from the original enlistment terms for an application for the North-West Mounted Police in 1873.

"Candidates must be active, able bodied men of thoroughly sound constitution and exemplary character. They should be able to ride well, etc., etc."

In those early days, the young Force did not have the time, the staff nor the facilities for the advanced cavalry training that developed later. The originals were expected to be able to ride and care for horses when they enlisted; the majority could, but, as we see here there were exceptions.

Troop Officer, to Orderly Constable: "Damn it all, I've told these chaps over and over, not to show off on horseback, especially in front of the Indians."

Blackfoot Brave in background: "Me think he no show off; *me* think **samaganis* no can ride horse."

*Samaganis — the Indian word for policeman, or literally "pony soldier."

FROM THE GENESIS of the Force, housing and equipment for personnel has always been a problem. The vast majority of members who were constables or N.C.O.'s brought their brides too and raised families in such surroundings! No plumbing (outhouses, or privies only), no running water.

My valiant young wife raised three children, pumped water in the summer and melted ice in the winter, on prairie detachments. A city girl by upbringing, the sight of her first Mounted Police residence with its wooden backhouse left her speechless, but she complained not! In the summer, I preceded her to this little edifice, stamping on the board walk to chase away the rats. In winter, I did likewise to break trail in drifted snow.

Another common practice in the rigid economy of the dear old Force was to billet single men in the spare room of married quarters. Fortunately most compassionate commanding officers frowned upon this stupid government economy. But Win (my wife) and I did experience this situation in one outpost.

Other Force families however, in many midwest posts, suffered the added "inconvenience" of having an iron cell or single gaol positioned in one room of their dwelling. Here on many a long weekend night, a drunken prisoner would howl and curse the night away, keeping the constable's wife and children in a state of fretful and sometimes fearful awakeness.

In spite of this, the policeman's wife often made breakfast or lunch for the sobered inmate who would be shamed into tearful gratitude and, because he enjoyed her cooking so much, would soon endeavour to get himself arrested again!

That was the way it was, right up until the middle and late forties and later, in some parts. But if we thought it was bad, let me quote from an ancient report by North-West Mounted Police Commissioner L. W. Herchmer, addressed to the government in Ottawa, December 1888: "I regret extremely to have to again call your attention to the wretched barracks furniture now in possession of the Force. This, the finest body of men in the country, still sleep on boards and trestles, while the prisoners in the gaols have neat iron cots."

Fortunately there is such a thing called progress and as a result, the conditions described no longer exist in the Force.

PARADE — ATTENTION!

THE INSPECTING Sub-Division Officer Commanding and his Patrol Sergeant, step into the little crowded three-man detachment office, to carry out 'Detachment Inspection'.

Patrol Sergeant: "PARADE, — ATTEN — SHUN." (The frame structure vibrates with the crash of long boots and heavy bodies coming to attention.)

Inspector: (Deafened by the mighty voice of the Sergeant) "Please, Sergeant, that's enough; stand them at ease."

Patrol Sergeant: "PARADE — STAND AT — EEEEZZ."

To those of us who experienced this sort of thing in some of the little one-office, tumble-down, out-post detachments, the absurdity, the parody of a parade ground inspection in such an environment, with foot stomping and saluting, will be appreciated.

I recall one little building containing a small office in which five of us were drilled, shoulder to shoulder, marking time, halting, etc., until the dust from the board ceiling showered down on our Review Order uniforms.

Not all officers of course would follow the regulations with such zeal; nor would they go through the whole *Manual of Small Arms* drill, but rather content themselves and everyone else with checking the cash book, the files, counting the equipment and checking it off the QM stores ledger. Those were the days!

THE UNMUSICAL RIDE

NEVER A TRUE LOVER OF HORSES in the sense of riding for pleasure, I nonetheless received more than a share of cavalry training and rode for two years in various mounted troop duties — including a major riot! Again, later in northern Saskatchewan, two winters of mounted patrols served to *widen* the gulf between the horse and me. There were, of course, moments of equestrian enjoyment, such as galloping at top speed over a good stretch of prairie.

Mounted patrol fundamentally involved discomfort, hard work, black flies and mosquitoes. Finishing a forty mile ride, you could *not* drive the beast into a garage and shut the door! The steed had to be dried, walked, watered and fed. The livery barn owner *had* to be paid; thereafter, *you* could find a bed!

This cartoon portrays a member's *dilemma* during a patrol in the Peace River country of northern Alberta, where I was stationed 1949 to 1951. Constable A. Soarbottom, late of "Musical Ride" fame, ruminates on the vanished city lights, girl friends and fickle fate.

While on the subject of this northern country my father, the late James W. Spalding, was Acting Sergeant-Major of the famous Peace River Trail Patrol of the Royal North-West Mounted, in 1905. He was a wonderful man and, unlike his son, was an expert horseman. He, together with about 28 other men of the Royal North-West Mounted Police were assigned by the government to build a road through the wilderness from Fort St. John, B.C., to the Yukon. Travelling hundreds of miles with pack horses and wagons they felled trees, cleared underbrush, built bridges and shelters and corduroyed muskeg. In two years of back-breaking labour, these policemen carved a good road 357 miles long from Fort St. John to Fort Graham and beyond!

Political vagaries stopped the almost completed work in 1907 after incredible problems and hardships had been endured and overcome.

In 1941, under the pressure and urgency of World War II, the Americans came in and built the *now* famous Alaska Highway, portions of which followed the *original* route surveyed by the R.N.W.M.P. This was a monumental piece of road building by comparison. But there *was* a difference. They employed *thousands* of men and used *every conceivable* type of machinery; with *unlimited* funds! *Sic transit gloria.*

30

SWORD PLAY

THE BACKGROUND FOR THESE TWO ILLUSTRATIONS, "Sword Play" and "The Defaulter" lay in an eastern division of the Force, at a time when I was a lance corporal serving on detachment.

First a brief comment about the higher ranks of the R.C.M.P. Commissioned officers are required to purchase their own uniforms upon receiving their appointment. In addition to the actual clothing, such items as a gold braided belt, shoulder boards, cape, Sam Browne belt and sword with both steel and leather scabbards, are a must. These requirements stem from the semi-military cavalry background of the Force. In my view, and indeed that of many of my contemporaries, the sword is or was an archaic military weapon, and although traditionally considered to be the badge of a gentleman, was extremely out-of-date and had no place in equipment essential to a modern police force. However, in the era embracing this incident, I was not involved in officers' status symbols.

For the past forty years at least, very few of the commissioned ranks of the Royal Canadian Mounted Police in any part of Canada encountered those extremely formal or ceremonial occasions, wherein they must turn out in full dress which would actually necessitate the wearing of the sword with steel scabbard. Neither was it a matter of great frequency where an officer would be ordered to appear on an inspection parade, clad in Review Order or Service Dress, wearing his sword in the leather scabbard, and either mounted or dismounted. I should add the standard exception here, which is at the Regina Training Depot, where officers parade regularly with troops in training.

Indeed, many officers of the Force have passed their entire career of thirty-five years without having worn the sword more than a half dozen times; some, never.

Many of us had been called in from surrounding detachments to headquarters, where together with the local personnel we were to be drilled because of the forthcoming inspection by the deputy commissioner from Ottawa.

The time of most commissioned officers in the Force is consumed with administrative, command and supervisory duties. Since there are only two semi-military establishments, Regina, and Ottawa, there is little requirement outside these points for officers or other ranks of the R.C.M.P. for that matter, to be engaged in ceremonial or other drill exhibitions.

When the morning for the formal inspection arrived, we of the ranks had already been immersed in many hours of marching, countermarching, foot and arms and sundry square bashing exercises; we were, by then, in pretty good shape to stand scrutiny. Not so the poor officers. They had been engrossed in their routine duties right up to inspection time but of course, being officers, they were expected to know all things at all times.

The gentlemen in question, five in number, appeared on the parade square in full Review Order, which consisted of scarlet tunic, stetson, breeches, riding boots, Sam Browne belt, sword frog and sword in leather scabbard. They took up positions most conspicuously in front of each platoon. All they had to do really was to obey the commands of the senior officer, draw swords, salute when the general order was given, then return swords to the sheath on command "Order Arms". However, if one has *not* practiced sheathing and unsheathing a sword for a long time, one is apt to forget that there is a right and wrong way to return a sword to its scabbard; done the *wrong* way, it will go in only *partially* and if forced, will *stick*, becoming most difficult to extricate!

All went well, until the command "Order Arms" the signal for us other ranks to ground-butt our rifles, and the officers to return swords to scabbards. The results were catastrophic; the four platoon commanders struggled manfully with the cursed swords which went in the *wrong* way!

We in the ranks were convulsed with laughter, *silently* of course; the unuttered profanity of the commissioned ranks could be *felt* rather than heard, and their angry scarlet faces reflected the red glow of their tunics.

That evening in barracks, I completed the cartoon of the day's display, passed it around to some of the troops and then dismissed it from my mind. They all had a good laugh, especially at the obscene and profane blurbs I had interjected over the head of each caricatured officer, concerning what and where they would *like* to put the swords in question. This was a *fatal* addition to the drawing! (The one you see here has been *greatly* modified.)

Next morning, preparing to leave for home, I received a summons to appear before the Sergeant-Major. Such an event in the life of a junior ranking mounted policeman strikes a coldness to the heart with a feeling of impending doom. On my way to the office of this august person, my mind ranged over *every* situation, *except* the cartoon; was it a transfer, a bad report, dirty buttons, dirty car? I mentally eliminated them one by one. Reporting, the Sergeant-Major promptly informed me I was under open *arrest* and marched me into the office of the Sub-Division Commander, who was one of the officers who had been on parade, and who by his height was quickly identifiable in the drawing. This gentleman fixed me with a baleful glare, then thrust the sheet of paper bearing the cartoon under my nose.

"Is this your work, Corporal?"

"Yes, Sir," I replied, "But . . . "

"No but's about it; you should be ashamed of yourself, a non-commissioned officer in the Mounted Police, and the son of a former officer of this Force, and if I recall aright, with the reputation of a strict disciplinarian; this is disgraceful . . . "

The enormity of my crime *now* dawned upon me. Standing rigidly at attention, my hands were wet and I could feel beads of sweat on my forehead (other ranks sweat, as they say; only officers perspire).

Utterly cowed, I was ordered to appear before the Division Commander the following morning at 10:00 a.m. for Orderly Room (a form of summary court martial).

THE DEFAULTER

AFTER A BLACK NIGHT of fitful sleep, next morning saw me standing before the supreme commander's door, in red serge, breeches and boots, minus spurs, hat and belt, a traditional form of penance before trial. The roaring command of the Sergeant-Major nearly shattered my eardrums, and I was marched forward through the open door to within a few inches of the C.O.'s desk — "MARK TIME, — HALT" bellowed the Sergeant-Major.

Number, name, and rank were rattled off, and exhibit one was placed on the Commander's desk with all its humiliating characteristics, and discernible caricatures of the officers concerned.

The Assistant Commissioner adjusted his glasses calmly and stared down as if at some revolting object. My mind pictured his growing horror at this gross insubordination. There was what authors like to describe as a "pregnant silence" broken only by the Sergeant-Major's heavy breathing behind my ear and the loud, slow ticking of the government issue office clock on the wall which read 10:30 a.m.

To the utter amazement of all and especially your obedient servant, the Commanding Officer smiled, and then chuckled for just a few seconds, then he glanced up at me, the prisoner at the bar, but now his face was set, his glance cold, eyes penetrating; there was no smile. He did not read out the charge, nor ask me to plead to it.

"I presume you intended this, this, ah . . . picture for barrack room consumption only?" he asked. "Yes, Sir," I replied.

"It seems obvious to me that one of your admiring comrades showed this around somewhat far afield, whether by accident or design is a matter of conjecture . . . " The C.O. glanced again at the cartoon.

"You have a good record thus far, Spalding. Don't spoil it. I'm familiar with your flair for drawings and your sense of humour, however misdirected in this case. As for the charge of insubordination, I do not intend to adhere to the letter of the law. But your choice of subject, time and place was unwise; such action is not in the best interest of police discipline, nor your own. Remember, the pen is not only mightier than the sword, it can frequently be more dangerous. Go and sin no more!" (or words to that effect). The Assistant Commissioner then dismissed the charge.

36

TOWN PATROL

THIS DRAWING was made for the *R.C.M.P. Quarterly* some years ago. I have re-drawn it for this production because of several requests.

During the depression, many small towns in western Canada were financially unable to support their own municipal police forces and as a consequence, entered into contractual obligations with the federal government whereby a member or members of the Mounted Police were assigned to carry out the necessary policing duties.

In many of the smaller towns this was a boring, monotonous (and in the view of many members) a completely demeaning task unworthy of a disciplined semi-military body such as the Force.

However this was not a majority opinion, and it definitely did not include the feelings of the citizens of the towns in question. On the contrary, they began to find themselves the recipients of very reassuring police protection and efficiency far superior to that performed by an untrained person who often had to double as fireman, town dog-catcher and janitor as well as lawman.

THIS IS ONE OF MY ORIGINAL CARTOONS which I have not retouched or revised. It depicts a room in barracks in old "C" Block, Regina, Saskatchewan.

These old barracks rooms were cold and draughty, and when blizzard conditions prevailed, the fine powdered snow would blow in around the windows and form tiny drifts on the sills and floor. In the hot dry summers of the "Dirty Thirties," instead of powdered snow it was fine dust.

Each of the rooms would accommodate twelve to fifteen men and more, depending on the influx of recruits. All articles of uniform, clothing and kit had to be stowed in a prescribed manner on the shelf and wall back of each bed. Surplus blankets were rolled tightly around extra sheets, which were set into a compact square with their edges facing out. This bedroll was placed at the head of the bed when it was not being occupied by the recruit. White kit bag and stable boots were placed at the foot under the bed. No item of civilian wear was permitted to be exposed in the barracks rooms. The only extra piece of equipment allowed was a small single drawer table in which to keep boot brushes and toilet articles.

In spite of the discomfort and sometimes crowded conditions, it was a man's world. I can still smell the saddle soap, the boot polish and leather but above all, the pervading clean odour of horse.

THE MUSICAL ROSE MARIE, and sundry Hollywood glamour shows of stage and screen in the late twenties and thirties, portrayed life in the Royal Canadian Mounted in terms of sweet romance and corny unbelievable adventure.

For years Mounted Policemen recoiled with embarrassment at the Rose Marie theme songs, especially "Here come the Mounties, like a pack of angry wolves on the trail." The ghost of Commissioner French must have wept!

As a result of this famous show, various detachment posts across the country known for their lack of heavy work load, became "Rose Marie Detachments." Certain types of men in the outfit endowed with good looks and physique and imbued with a sense of their own importance, were tagged "Nelson Eddie's."

But the Mounted Policeman clad in full Review Order uniform, paddling a canoe on a wilderness river with a scantily clad musical star, need I say, it just *never* was!

THE TRUMPETERS

A VANISHED BREED in the Royal Canadian Mounted, is the "boy trumpeter." Such have been engaged by the Force since its inception. They were abolished at the outset of World War II.

The starting ages of these recruits varied from sixteen to eighteen years of age. They took part in regular basic training, but were not assigned to field duties until they had come of age.

The last of the trumpeters, whom I knew personally, were Tom Fell, Roy Sparrow, George Cutting, Alexander Mackenzie (later to distinguish himself through World War II service with the Seaforth Highlanders, and The Black Watch with the rank of Captain, and is now Sir Alexander Mackenzie) and last but not least, my old friend Ralph Carriere, who also served later with the Canadian Army (R.C.M.P.) Provost Corps overseas, and recently retired as Deputy Commissioner of the Force. They were a hardy lot, these young trumpet blowers, and their hours of duty in the barracks at Regina were long and hard on the wind. All through each day they blew calls which ranged from Reveille, Stables, Feed, the Quarter Hour, Fall In, Last Post and Lights Out, with many others in between, the names of which I have long forgotten.

The British cavalry Reveille was perhaps the longest and most beautiful sounding of all, but also the most hated, particularly in the dark winter mornings.

In the accompanying picture we see a portion of a long line of recruits on early morning stable parade (6:30 a.m.). They are dressed in brown canvas fatigues, forage hats, and ankle boots. Each man has a small denim bag tucked under his right arm. This contained the grooming kit which consisted of a curry comb, a dandy brush, a circular metal rough comb and a hoof pick.

The trumpeter is blowing the Stable Call, which will be a signal to the N.C.O. to march 'em off to the horse lines.

First rookie: "I know what I'd like to do with his — **!!!!*** — horn."
Second rookie: "Don't say it, the very thought hurts me."

44

STABLE DAZE

HERE IS ANOTHER OF THE VANISHED SEGMENTS of tradition and, in this instance, the training environment of the R.C.M.P. Depicted here is a duty which was known by several colourful names, most of them unprintable, but officially as Stable Orderly. Each weekend, and during the evening hours, two or more members were assigned to the five wooden stables housing anywhere from fifty to seventy-five horses; in earlier days a hundred. The tour of duty was from Reveille, 6:00 a.m., until 8:00 p.m. They had to attend to the perpetual cleanliness and security of the stables and the horses, and on holidays to see that they were fed three times a day.

One did not mind mid-week assignments of this nature, but to draw weekend Stable Orderly was a bitter pill.

An added fillip with all this bodily contact and intimate association with the horse and his or its environment, was the *smell*; it never left one, even on a Saturday night in town. One never had to tell the girl friend about one's occupation. Oddly enough though, they did *not* seem to mind! Whenever some finicking recruit would *whine* about the odour of horse and stable a "rough riding" corporal would tell him in *colourful* language that he smelled *like* a man!

Many the hour have we put in at Regina, and later in Rockcliffe, Ontario (the latter a former Eastern Training Depot), pushing the old wheelbarrow, shoving the stable broom and manicuring the hooves of our omnipresent equine comrades. (They had regimental numbers *too*, you know.)

EQUITATION, LITERALLY, "horsemanship" and as an equitant (one who straddles a horse), we of the vintage spent most of our training days acquiring posterior anatomies of the consistency and toughness of old leather after, of course, an initial period of raw beef entrée.

In my personal view the decision to abolish the maintenance of the horse as a training medium was a sad day for the Mounted Police. (This occurred in the late sixties, many years after I had ceased to bash my rear in the saddle.)

Staff Sergeant Cecil Walker expressed the effect most eloquently in an article he wrote entitled *L'Esprit Cavalier*.

Not because I loved horses, nor because I had carried out working police patrols in the saddle. It was my conviction that the saddle horse bred and developed by and for the Mounted Police (at Fort Walsh, Saskatchewan) was and is one of the finest training aids in existence. In the shape of this big, powerful and sometimes dangerously temperamental animal, the recruit was confronted with a flesh and blood creature which he had to master, then establish a rapport through the exercise of superior will, physical control and no little amount of courage. In other words, equitation embodied everything which can be produced in physical training and all the mechanical aids that go with it.

Possibly transcending this is the additional factor which embraces morale. Mounted training placed the R.C.M.P. recruit a cut above all other services. It engendered an elan, a sense of achievement and pride, as well as a feeling of comradeship.

The cartoon on this sport depicts an incident which actually happened and is indicative of the high state of excitement developed by the horses. The little mare in question could hardly contain herself and aggressively leaped up onto the ball in order (apparently) to speed up the forward motion.

The next drawing shows the Balaklava Melee. This particular play has been a part of British Cavalry training for decades. Each team of four, or six, mounted men wear helmets similar to fencing masks, the crown of each being surmounted by a loosely attached feather (different colour for each team). The object is to knock the feather off the helmet of the opposing team member with a four-foot bamboo truncheon. This is a relatively harmless weapon unless one happens to receive a smack across the bare arms, shoulders or hands.

All of these mounted sports constituted an extension of the actual cavalry drill and equitation training. But additionally they provided a tremendous outlet of energy for strong and healthy young men and engendered a spirit of competition and good sportsmanship.

There is also another facet of mounted training not found in any other type of physical drill. This is in the form of mounted games and competitions.

Here we found that our horses entered into the spirit with as much, and often a greater zest, than the riders.

I have endeavoured to portray some of these on the next few pages in a humourous light. In order of preference dictated by the riding masters at Regina, they were Jumping, Tent Pegging, Roman Riding, Push Ball and the famous Balaklava Melee. Tent pegging could be done with either the sword or the lance, and was probably the most thrilling of the lot from a spectator viewpoint. Here, man and horse became one. The rider, sometimes clad in boots and breeches with white singlet, Stetson hat and long lance, or in full dress scarlet, pushed his mount on signal into a dead gallop, gradually bringing his lance down to the "attack" position, and aiming it as truly as possible at a wooden peg, driven at an angle into the ground ahead of him. The object is to spear the peg, and lift it from the ground intact, and carry it on the tip of the lance to the end of the run. It's quite a feat and requires the utmost co-ordination between rider and mount.

Push Ball was played with a gigantic, leather, air-filled ball, not unlike a giant soccer ball. It stood about as high as a horse's withers. Four or six men to a side participated. The object, to manoeuvre the ball by making the horses push it with their chest and knees towards and eventually through, the football field goal posts.

RED COAT, RED FACE

I MADE THIS DRAWING FROM AN OLD PHOTO taken in 1933 while I was on a special detail to search for a group of prospectors, supposed to be overdue.

The scene is on board an Eskimo whaling boat in the eastern Arctic, near Hudson Strait. We had been hunting white whale and seal for a couple of days, and had just shot the Hair seal (weight about one thousand pounds) which the Eskimo family urgently needed for food and clothing.

In this little vessel there were six men and five women and a couple of husky dogs. My companion and myself were the only white men.

The Eskimos used to be greatly puzzled and amused by our prudish efforts at some semblance of modesty when it was necessary for us to respond to the urges of nature.

Here, one of the Eskimo women is saying to your blushing artist, "Not into the wind big boy . . . "

THE VIGIL
Or 3:00 a.m. and No C.I.B.

MANY OF US HAVE PERFORMED THIS DUTY from time to time on the rural detachments. Here we see a junior member, Constable A. Flutter, guarding the scene of the crime next to the *corpus delecti* (covered with the blanket).

Constable Flutter has been thus assigned by his corporal who left with the police car to go to the nearest phone (thirty miles away) to put in a call for C.I.B. (Criminal Investigation Branch) assistance, in what has proven to be foul play. The corporal left a little before midnight; it is now 3:00 a.m., and, as the title goes, no C.I.B.

To the uninitiated, raw police recruit, a night spent alone under these circumstances, was always slightly unnerving.

I well remember being left to guard the bodies of two murdered people late one night. It was not in an old house, but rather on the open prairie. The night was warm and close; scudding dark clouds from time to time obscured the moon and fitfully cast grim shadows. Just before dawn, when the night is always blackest, it began to rain then settled into a steady downpour. The police party with the famous C.I.B. did not arrive until around 9:00 a.m., having become mired in good old prairie gumbo on the return trip.

There was an exchange of colourful language by all of us. The sergeant, however, who was a bit of a scholar, said reprovingly to me — *Do the duty that lies nearest thee* — GOETHE.

56

FROM ITS INCEPTION the Force has continually been called upon to do the spade work for many federal government departments in terms of general inquiries, data gathering, and investigations.

For many years one of the annual form-filling demands from Ottawa was the securing of a head count of the numbers of various species of migratory birds and animals. One of the most persistent statistical requests from the seat of brain power involved counting the Snowshoe Rabbit or Varying Hare. I never did have time to find out which was which, or were the twain one!

Here we have a picture of Constable I. M. A. Awk of "K" Division, after many arduous miles of canoe and foot patrol, locating his quarry. Constable Awk is in the act of photographing the rare striped bellied Woofer Cock. In inclement weather, it flies backwards crying woof woof! to keep the wind out of its eyes.

OH, LOCHINVAR!

FROM TIME IMMEMORIAL, well at least since 1882 (the year that Regina became the headquarters and training centre of the Mounted Police) young recruits have squired and courted the pretty and sometimes seductive ladies of the Queen City.

Here we look in on a very green recruit, fresh from the cloistered suburbs of metropolitan Toronto. They have just returned to her apartment from the R.C.M.P. Regimental Ball at the barracks.

Recruit: "And if I'm able to ride him well enough, I may get a transfer to the Musical Ride at — "

Lady of the Night: "Oh for the love of Dumont, quit talking about your smelly old horse, and show me some of that police-brutality."

MY FRIEND TRUMPETER GEORGE CUTTING was an extraordinary lad; physically tough, cocky and afraid of nothing except possibly the Post Sergeant-Major. One bitter winter morning in Regina, George rose as usual minutes before reveille blowing time, whereupon he would normally dress in uniform, go outside of the barrack block to the front of the administration building known as "A" Block, and tootle the call.

This particular morning the wind was howling, and the thermometer registered twenty below. He took one look at the dark, cold barrack square and said "to hell with it." So this enterprising trumpeter threw open the window on the first landing in "C" Block and, clad only in his long winter underwear, placed trumpet to lips, leaned out and blew reveille.

Unfortunately he did not notice the Division Sergeant-Major, who was Orderly Officer of the Day, ascending the stairway behind him. The S.-M. graciously waited until Cutting had finished then, as the last notes of the call faded, he brought his stout riding crop down across George's taut posterior. All the sympathy poor Cutting got from us "old timers" in barrack room five was group hilarity and the offer of horse liniment.

THE HEAVING BOSOM of the vast and timeless ocean never had any romantic appeal for me, except or unless viewed from a staunch rock-bound shoreline. The situation in the cartoon here, depicted yours truly on some of my thankfully infrequent trips in the ships and with the gallant men of the R.C.M.P. Marine Service. This particular scene was set in the North Atlantic, an excellent environment in which one who is subject to *mal de mer*, can think up ways to "sink the ship, Master Gunner, split her in twain." For days afterwards, the even solid earth reeled under me.

Oddly though, my youngest son served four years in the R.C.M.P. Marine Division, and my eldest has been and still is, an Officer in Her Majesty's Canadian Navy, for over sixteen years now. Neither of them complained too much about the roll of waters but were grateful that they had not inherited their father's seasick genes.

PERSONNEL PROBLEMS

ONE OF THE FUNDAMENTAL DUTIES of the Personnel Officer was that of counselling the more junior members of the Force with respect to their personal difficulties. Let us look in on this dialogue which takes place in the Training Depot at Regina.

Division Personnel Officer: "Ahem, now then Constable Greef, I see by the record you are a member of the senior 'Cock of the Walk' troop. The elite recruits of the Depot, ha ha!"

Recruit Constable Greef: "Yes that's right sir. You must know how hard we have to work to get into that Squad; sixteen, eighteen hours a day."

Personnel Officer: "Of course, go on please."

Constable: "Well, — ah, — I can hardly talk about this sir."

Personnel Officer: "Come, come man, brace up now, speak out!"

Constable, overcome with emotion: (Sob) " — well, I — I — have a girl friend, but I've been so darn tired at night, I can't spend much time with her — and . . . "

Personnel Officer: "So? — go on man!"

Constable: "Well, *(sob)*, the other night, she — she — she said to me —*(groan)*, she said, 'If you're *Cock of the Walk*, you'd better start making like a rooster, or I'm getting myself a new cat'."

Personnel Officer: "Egad, I'm so sorry, what did you say her name was?"

NO COMPLAINTS

AH, THE SWEET BLISS — the absolute ambrosia of mountain air, and in no other place than British Columbia — well almost.

Members of the R.C.M.P. were subject to transfer more frequently than any other service, which included some very isolated stations which were not always in the Territories or the Arctic.

Personnel, single or married, often traversed this country from coast to coast, north to south many times during their years of active duty. I for example, was transferred twenty-one times, and lived in twenty-seven different married establishments, during thirty-six years in the Force.

Naturally many postings are preferred over others, and then there are some which one hopes one will never be sent to. But British Columbia is certainly a favoured spot by most members of the Force.

Here in this cartoon, we see Corporal Chinook and Constable Coho, native sons of the coast province who, after fifteen years of duty in other parts of the nation are, at last, unexpectedly transferred to their home and native land!

(Personally, I liked Nova Scotia just as much.)

COMMISSIONER L. H. NICHOLSON, M.B.E., LL.D., shown in this sketch was the ninth Commissioner of the Royal Canadian Mounted Police, serving in that capacity from 1951 to 1959. I was privileged to serve under him as head of the Force's Personnel Branch, 1951 to 1956.

Nicholson was held in very high regard by all ranks of the Mounted Police. His personality is reflected in his compassion, warmth and good humour. Commissioner Nicholson retired with honour and dignity in 1959, and his loss was keenly felt by all of us.

This drawing carries a little ironic humour which will be recognized by those who served with him. In this imaginary situation we see the Commissioner making the rounds of the R.C.M.P. Headquarters just prior to his departure, saying farewell to some members. He is speaking to the staff artist.

Commissioner Nicholson: "Tell me, how did you conceive, or who gave you the idea to do a seascape of Newfoundland, for my retirement gift?"

INSPECTION — REGINA BARRACKS

A TRADITIONAL RITUAL in the Royal Canadian Mounted Police Barracks at Regina, Saskatchewan, since the 1880's was the Saturday morning inspection by the Commanding Officer.

All Friday night, well at least until "Lights Out," those in the rank and file were confined to barracks to scrub and wax floors, polish door knobs, muck out the stables, set up bed kits and clean personal equipment.

Early Saturday, the final hours were consumed with much scurrying, touching up and, on the part of junior n.c.o.'s, double checking everything. Members completing their various assigned fatigue duties would hurry back to the respective posts to don full dress — anyone caught out of position by the time the inspection team started rounds was dead, figuratively speaking.

The temporary peace was suddenly shattered by a blast from the cavalry trumpet sounding the "General Inspection Call," and at precisely 11 : 00 a.m. the great oak doors of "A" Block would bang open and, like cuckoos from a clock, out would march the "Holy Three." First, the Divisional Sergeant-Major, then the Commanding Officer, then the adjutant, followed lastly by the "note-book bearer," the Division Orderly. They tramped in single file throughout the entire performance and, to me, (Commissioners and Deputies forgive please) it was the funniest sight in the world.

The Regina "Depot" Division cantonment is a big place but on this day, as it was every week, the inspection was meticulous. Heaven help the rookie with dirty buttons or improperly made bed. And speaking of beds, one of the hilarious gestures of the Adjutant (well, one Adjutant anyway), was to strike the heavy, tautly drawn blanket bed covering of every third or fourth bed in the rows. If dust rose in little puffs, the D.O. (Division Orderly) scribbled the man's name and number in his little black book. The ludicrous part of this action was that prairie dust was a part of the whole scene, especially in those dry years.

Years later, when I became a commissioned officer, I was posted to "Depot" and as fate would punish a humourist and cartoonist, I was to become a part of this Saturday inspection ritual for just on three years!

THE R.C.M.P. TRAINING COMPLEX at Regina, Saskatchewan, is the recruit processing and indoctrination centre for the whole Force. It was thus established in 1882, and also as the headquarters for the Mounted Police. The administrative headquarters was moved to Ottawa, the nation's capital, in 1920.

The "Depot" as it is known throughout the service, is unique in terms of its para-military complexion embracing a large police force. It is, of course, a fact of progress that the famous old wooden riding schools and stables have long gone, and noble horses too. But the training and discipline, while modified and modernized with vastly improved techniques, remains tough and exacting.

Quite apart from the regular subjects taught in the R.C.M.P. training syllabus, such as law (criminal code and federal statutes), fingerprinting, plan drawing, etc., there are in excess of forty subjects. There is included here the broad subject of police community relations. This embraces topics such as youth and youth problems, alcohol education, social mobility, the psychology of human development, deviant behaviour patterns, perception and interpersonal relations. These lectures are given by qualified professional people.

If for any reason, political, social or what-have-you, the Force is compelled to abandon its careful screening and selection of recruits, and its high standard of discipline, it will cease to exist as Canada's finest.

Now for a bite of humour with some contemporary jargon. Don't ask me how the very long haired bearded chap got into the dress uniform, and escaped the Post barber, just put it down to *artist's license.*

Here we see the Training Officer, the Depot Sergeant-Major, a Drill Instructor Corporal and the new Trainee.

New bearded recruit: "Peace man; this pad is really groovy, it's a gas. Which one of you cats do I rap with when I want to split to town?"

Training Officer to over-wrought Sergeant-Major: "Come now Sergeant-Major, you must learn to communicate in meaningful dialogue with the contemporary activist personality, and acquire a participatory attitude."

Rapidly departing Corporal: "I'm going to split before the S.-M. digs."

CORPORAL HARDGUTZ, veteran of many arduous patrols and a junior constable on his first northern assignment who has been plying the n.c.o. with many questions.

Hardgutz: "No, Constable Quiry, we do not feed the huskies *Doctor Ballies Pink Poodle Vitamin Yummies!*"

COMMISSIONER GEORGE B. MCCLELLAN, the twelfth Commissioner of the R.C.M.P. (1963-1967). Upon his retirement he accepted the position of Ombudsman for the Province of Alberta, the first such appointment in Canada. The tremendous success McClellan has achieved in this role with two different elected governments of that province, has given the lie to the comments of cynics and wiseacres. These were quick to pronounce that a policeman would be entirely unsuited to such a task. They exposed their abysmal ignorance of the role of police in our society, especially that of the R.C.M.P.

Apart from being a raconteur of humorous stories, McClellan was also a connoisseur of western art, specifically the work of the famous American "cowboy" painter, Charles M. Russell.

In this illustration, we see the former Commissioner on one of his annual inspection trips into the northwest, and at one of the more remote and primitive detachments. He is questioning the lone constable "in charge" on his general knowledge.

Commissioner: "Now Constable Outback, tell me what you know about Charles M. Russell."

Constable: "Oh, Ah, yes sir, — now let me see — oh he must be one of our *Ten Most Wanted Men,* Sir?"

Commissioner departs in a dejected state.

IT HAS BEEN SAID AT TIMES that the police are too self conscious. In this there is probably a degree of truth. Nevertheless the law enforcement bodies are constantly being reminded to enhance their reputations, and renew their "image."

Regardless of what they do in this field, the daily press continues to use these old cliches, just a few of which I have drawn here.

HEAVILY ARMED POLICE   I've never seen a heavily armed policeman in my experience, even in the most intensive man-hunt.

CLUB SWINGING POLICE   Police never defend themselves, or fight off a mob of rioters; they are always reported by the press as "clubbing students" or swinging their clubs at the "protesters."

POLICE PROBER   Should be self explanatory.

There are many others used daily, on television, radio and in the papers, such as that old stand-by, "police brutality." Apparently *only* police can be brutal!

WILLIAM LEONARD HIGGITT became the fourteenth Commissioner of the Royal Canadian Mounted Police on October 1st, 1969. Commissioner Higgitt, born in Saskatchewan, joined the R.C.M.P. in 1937. I have known Len Higgit for over twenty years. Among many attributes he possesses a warm sense of humour and quick wit. I know he will forgive my attempt at cartooning him here with the big moustached Chief Superintendent Dick Stone, Commanding Officer of "Training Depot" at Regina, the scene of this drawing: Here they are reviewing a new squad of recruits.

Commissioner: "Great Riel's Ghost, Chief Superintendent Stone, where in — did she — did this rookie come from!"

C/S Stone: "Well sir, I thought you might like to get one jump ahead of er, Women's Lib."

Higgitt: "But that uniform Stone, isn't it rather . . . "

C/S Stone: "Oh I assure you sir, it's done wonders for morale."

Commissioner: "Hmm, well Stone, pending my decision, I think you'd better double the Night Guard around these barracks."

CONSTABLE CYRIL WHIFFENPOOF, five foot nine, weighing 155 pounds, has just been engaged in a tremendous struggle while arresting a man weighing 225 pounds, height six-foot, four inches. Here we see him telephoning the sub-division headquarters to advise of the situation.

Constable Whiffenpoof: *(puff, puff, gasp . . .)* "Sir, I've just arrested the Calgary Killer, wanted in seven provinces and twenty-nine states."

Voice from HQ: "Well now, I trust you did not forget the usual warning — you sound a little out of breath by the way."

Whiffenpoof: "Yes sir, we had quite a struggle . . . "

Voice: "Now I certainly hope you have not hurt him in any way; you know the regulations re the handling of prisoners . . . they are quite clear and exact; you must use no more force than is absolutely necessary . . . I hope you have not damaged any government property, the Standing Orders are quite specific about this kind of thing" . . . and so, on and on into the night . . .

AMONG THE MANY extra-curricular subjects and studies required of Mounted Police recruits in training are social amenities including table etiquette. We did not have the benefit of such refinements in the good old "horse days!" In fact our etiquette was reserved for the feeding of our impatient and hungry mounts, which if *not* done properly, might earn one a kick or a bite.

This cartoon consequently is strictly born of my imagination. The shoulder flash on the irate senior member, has also been invented by yours truly, and any resemblance to the modern environment in "Depot Division" is strictly coincidental.

Senior Member (standing) a self-styled Shakespearean: "Get thee hence, thou gorbellied lout, thou hast made thyself a hack in the presence of thy fellow yeomen. Present thyself to the Master-at-Arms!"

Stout Constable with spoon and bib: "Meaning what, pray?"

Senior Constable: "Get off your fat butt, remove that diaper around your neck and report to the Sergeant-Major, that's what!"

Badly mauled Ottawa Youth surveyor: "Dig this man, — all I said to this chick was, 'we wannta look into some of your areas' — like man she never let me finish, she creamed me like Joe Frazier — do your *Just Society* thing!"

Female complainant: "Right on — you do your thing *fuzz* and keep this creep outa my hair, or he'll get some more power of the people, like *Women People*!"

Worn R.C.M.P. Desk Sergeant: "Peace, please PEACE!"

Hard-nosed Patrol Sergeant: "What do you mean by conveying a *civilian* in a patrol car, and a *female* at that!"

Green young Constable: "Honest Sarge, I just stopped to warn her about getting into cars with strange men . . . when *zap*, I had it . . . just like that!"

CIVILIAN BRUTALITY

THOUGHT I'D MAKE A SWITCH in the headline here, just for a change of pace from the usual press cliche. Let us listen in on the trial.

Defence lawyer: "When this constable spoke to my client, his manner was very high-handed and rude, so my client called him a few names . . . "

Prosecutor: "Yes, your Honour, he called the constable an offspring of a dog, and a pig . . . "

Judge: "I don't see how he could be both . . . "

Prosecutor: "The accused proceeded to strike the constable with a tire iron, and inflicted the injuries you can see; it was at this juncture that the policeman struck him in the face with his fist."

Judge: "It matters not what provocation is used, the police constable over-reacted, we simply cannot have this kind of police brutality."

End of *Act One, Scene One.* The little fictional item above is not so far from the truth in actuality. Brutality is brutality regardless of the status of the individual in the social structure. It matters not whether he is a policeman, a soldier or civilian. But I have never read it in the press, or heard it on television, as military, civilian or if you will, professional brutality.

Well over sixty policemen (not cops) have been murdered in Canada since 1960; an uncounted number have been injured, some maimed for life at the hands of criminals. Society should ask, — "who is being brutal to whom?"

HAVING HAD THE MISFORTUNE to participate in three riots, one of major proportion, where one of our officers was killed, I have a distinct aversion to mobs. This attitude will disturb some ivory-insulated-desk-oriented-writers, when I augment this by stating that every protest march and assembly of any great number, is a potential mob, and a mob constitutes the explosive power for a riot. Because a mob does not think it is mindless; like a huge magnet it attracts to its periphery the lawless elements, the vandals and the looters.

Unfortunately, many judges and politicians do not seem to comprehend that a mob in spite of its mass and mindlessness, is controlled and directed in its embryo by one person or a small handful. These same members of our society, including some members of the press, also appear blind to the fact that no revolution or violent assault on constituted government was ever carried out by a majority, but always a small, intelligent but absolutely ruthless minority. It was President Lincoln who said in a speech relative to the Law, in Springfield, Illinois, 1838, I quote:

"If destruction be our lot, we ourselves be its author and finisher."

How terribly true today in North America, where freedom is rapidly becoming license to do anything or say anything. The democratic society does not seem to remember the lessons from Russia, Germany, Cuba, Algeria, Hungary and all the lesser "Iron Curtain" countries.

BELIEVE ME, no government department in Canada ever pampered and guarded their transport equipment with the passion devoted by the R.C.M.P. To dent a fender on a Mounted Police transport, puncture an aircraft pontoon, scrape the keel of a patrol boat, triggered investigation, multitudinous reports, statement and general inquiries.

All members therefore; young, old, long or short service, I'm sure, will understand the awful portent of this somewhat exaggerated cartoon!

PERHAPS THE SMALLEST, but certainly the hardest working "air force" in the Commonwealth, the Royal Canadian Mounted Police Air Division, created by Commissioner Sir James MacBrien in 1937, flies in all kinds of weather, all over Canada. From the high Arctic to Atlantic coast, across the prairies and over the rugged mountain terrain of British Columbia.

The men of the R.C.M.P. Air Division perform search and rescue (with very little publicity or acknowledgment). They convey prisoners, sick or injured woodsmen and members of the Force on sundry investigational duties and sometimes, V.I.P.'s. For example, in 1970, the R.C.M.P. Twin Otter, captained by Inspector A. F. Dye with Staff Sergeant Filiatrault and Special Constable R. F. Chapin conveyed Her Majesty the Queen, and H.R.H. the Duke of Edinburgh into the Canadian Arctic.

But the old Mounted Police MPG "Goose," winging the Canadian skies for over thirty years, is the veteran of the Force. The following cartoon illustrates.

Ottawa public relations type: "You don't mean to tell me we're going to fly to Whitehorse in this pregnant duck?"

Highly indignant R.C.M.P. Flight Sergeant: "Listen you — this is no pregnant duck! It's the R.C.M.P. Grumman twin engine amphibious *Goose*, CF-MPG. If your feet are too cold, then you can walk!"

IN THE BAD OLD DAYS, it was "murder most foul"; later "brutal murder"; still later, "gruesome murder."

But today, in this age of enlightenment and total freedom, the kill rate has risen in the North American continent to undreamed-of figures.

The acceptable excuses for murder now range from drug usage to alcohol to socio-political necessity. Family and sibling murder is now termed "domestic crime" or crime of passion. The utter fallacy of the present Canadian legal distinction between capital and non-capital murder should be apparent to any concerned person. Let us look in on this all-too-common street scene.

Arresting Constable: "Sorry mister, I have to arrest you; but don't worry, you'll be released on bail in a matter of hours. You'll have immediate access to legal aid. You have nothing to fear from any threat, although anything you say may be used as evidence. So you'd be wise to shut up."

Prisoner: "What'll I get for '*dis*, cop?"

Constable: "That's up to the Court; but don't be alarmed — you can't be hanged; you may get life, which of course means less than ten years, with parole perhaps in two. So cheer up old boy."

CONFESSIONAL FICTION

THE JULY 1972 ISSUE of Canada's great national magazine, *Maclean's* (not to be confused with the American phonetic enunciation, MacKLEENS), paid homage to a former R.C.M.P. corporal by way of a handsome colour plate cover and nearly thirteen pages, captioned in part, shattering a great Canadian legend. What legend? Contemporary language authorities define it as "a collection of lives of the Saints, stories and myths." Believe me, there are few saints in the Mounted Police, excepting perhaps *that* former corporal.

The only legends ever appended to the Force emanated from the fertile little heads of Hollywood's lurid fiction writers, and authors. They also invented the phoney motto "Get your Man" and "Mountie."

Is it not strange, that Canada's national magazine should produce these "Confessions" at a point in time when the Force stands on the threshold of its centennial? Singular too, that the "Mannix" of Saskatoon should have re-enlisted after some seven years with an organization whose leaders and system he so obviously despises.

Unquestionably there have been, and are, misfits, weaklings or incompetents within the Mounted Police for the simple reason that it is composed of human beings. But the percentage of such is minute, as is the scope of error by comparison with the size and complexity of operations.

Notwithstanding the fallibility of the human factor, the R.C.M.P. created a tradition and reputation in the service of the Canadian people unique in its versatility and efficiency.

On the lighter side for a moment, the cartoon opposite is entitled "Free at last" or *Aegrescit medendo.*

106

Corporal Drill Instructor: "Now then, pay attention men, — you are the last graduating troop for 1972. Soon you'll be going out to various postings all across Canada."

One Recruit: (sotto voice) "Amen."

Corporal: "Are you ready for the question?"

Troops: (muttering) "Lay it on man."

Corporal: "What is the most important thing you must remember for the coming year, 1973?"

One Recruit: "To renew my subscription to *Maclean's Magazine*, corporal."

(Exit one recruit under escort with one apoplectic corporal.)

SEX AND THE SINGLE MOUNTIE?

As far back as twenty years ago, the concept of a uniformed Women's Division of the Force was discussed. So it is not new in spite of recent press reports.

Here I have dreamed up what might be considered a really snappy uniform for the future Royal Canadian Mounted Women. In this dream, we see a veteran sergeant getting his first look at the new "rookie" while visiting the barracks square in Regina.

Sergeant: "Holy Walrus tusks — now I'd say that Ottawa has *really* produced a first class government issue — "

Young Constable: "Take it easy Sarge, she might be a member of *Women's Lib* — anyway you've just re-mustered for three *more* years of northern service!"